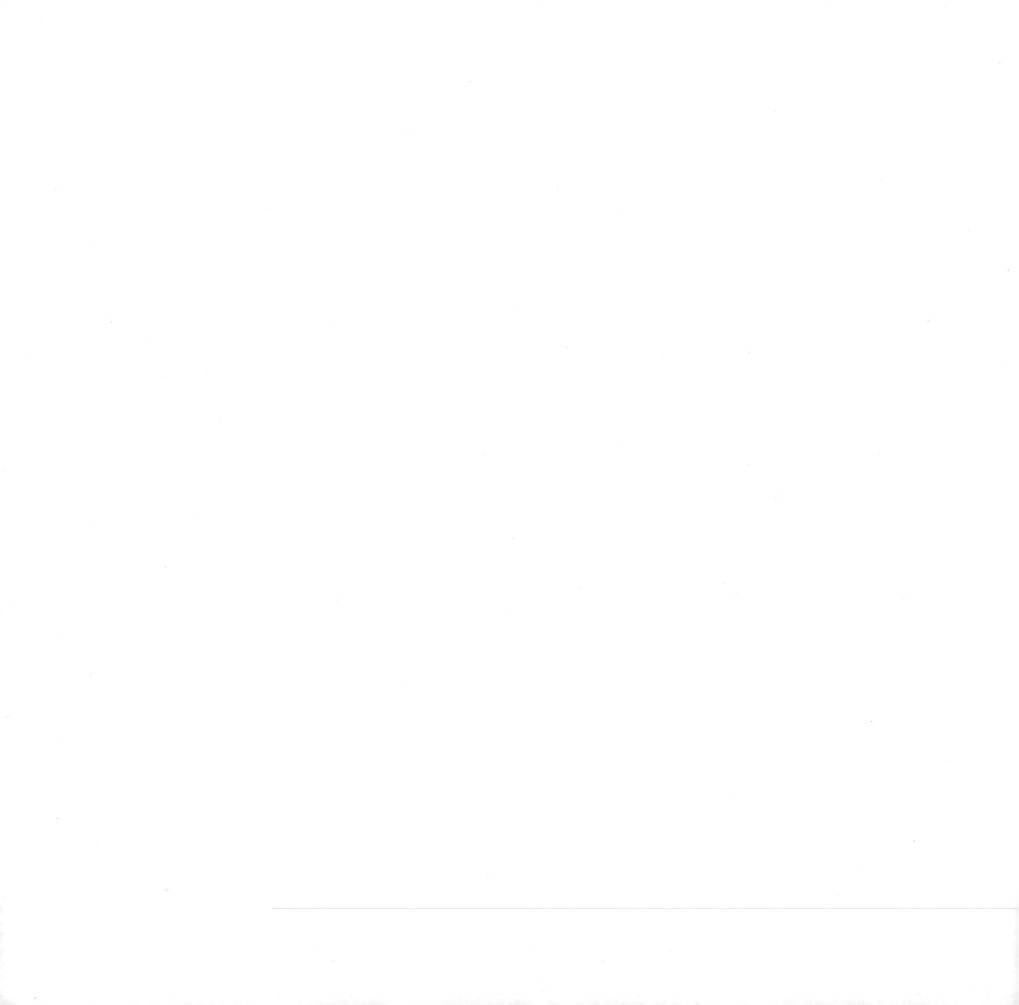

VANCOUVER WILD

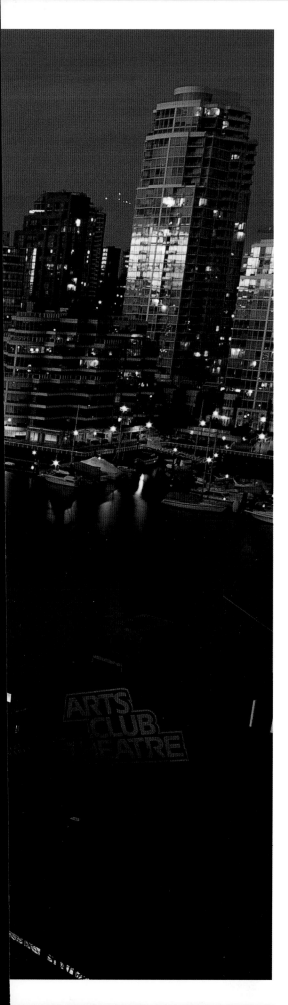

VANCOUVER WILD

A Photographer's Journey *through the*
Southern Coast Mountains

GRAHAM OSBORNE

text by RICHARD CANNINGS

GREYSTONE BOOKS

Douglas & McIntyre Publishing Group

Vancouver/Toronto/Berkeley

06 07 08 09 10   5 4 3 2 1

Greystone Books
A division of Douglas & McIntyre Ltd.
2323 Quebec Street, Suite 201
Vancouver, British Columbia
Canada V5T 4S7
www.greystonebooks.com

Library and Archives Canada Cataloguing in Publication
Osborne, Graham, 1962–
Vancouver wild : a photographer's journey through the southern Coast Moun-
tains / Graham Osborne ; text by Richard Cannings

ISBN-13: 978-1-55365-002-7 · ISBN-10: 1-55365-002-6

1. Natural History—British Columbia—Lower Mainland—Pictorial
works. 2. Natural history—British Columbia—Pictorial works. I. Cannings,
Richard J. (Richard James) II. Title.
QH106.2.B7082 2006   508.711´3´0222   C2006-900361-0

Editing by Nancy Flight
Jacket and text design by Naomi MacDougall
Jacket photographs by Graham Osborne
Map by Stuart Daniel
Printed and bound in China by C&C Offset Printing Co. Ltd.
Printed on acid-free paper

Distributed in the U.S. by Publishers Group West
We gratefully acknowledge the financial support of the Canada Council for
the Arts, the British Columbia Arts Council, and the Government of Canada
through the Book Publishing Industry Development Program (BPIDP) for
our publishing activities.

TO OUR SON,

Michael Kenneth Peter,

What a great blessing you are.

Love, Mom and Dad

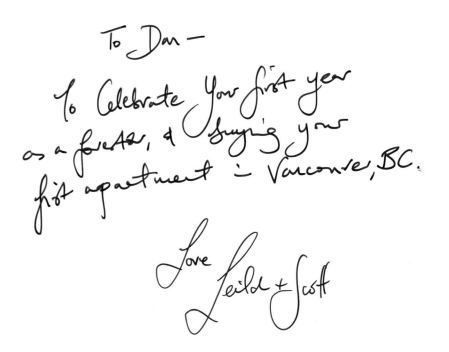

Christmas 2006

To Dan —

To Celebrate Your first year
as a forester, & buying your
first apartment in Vancouver, BC.

Love
Leila & Scott

*M*Y MIND GOES BACK TO BOYHOOD springs sometimes. Simple times. Knee-deep in a swamp next to our Tsawwassen home, croaking out my very best frog call. The hapless frog would invariably answer, and I would inch ever so slowly closer to my prize. At the right moment, I would lunge forward, seize the wriggling amphibian, and then plop him unceremoniously into the amphibian transport vessel (bucket). Back home, he would be released, lovingly, into the family aquarium—incarceration if you were to ask the frog.

There were garter snakes too, snatched neatly as they suntanned along the warm, brambled edge of an abandoned field. Later I would charge the neighbour kids ten cents to touch them (girls could just look if they wanted), and then I would slip them, squirming, back into my homemade snake pit.

A decade later, I would find myself returning to these childhood roots, studying zoology at the University of British Columbia. A series of family transfers had taken me to Ottawa and Washington, D.C., and being away had left me with a great longing for the west coast, for the grandness of nature that had surrounded me as I grew up.

I missed the tumbling freshets that cascaded out of the south Coast Range, the strong west wind that funneled up Howe Sound after a November storm, and the gentle twilight chorus of frogs in the nearby pond lands of Tsawwassen. I missed catching butterflies along Strawberry Flats in Manning Park and hiking the old blueberry burn to Nicomen Lake. And I missed the tangy seaweed smell of Boundary Bay at low tide, the aromatic crunch of lodgepole pinecones along the headwaters of the Skagit, and the honey-sweet smell of cottonwoods in spring as they carpeted the banks of the Fraser in a snowfall of downy tufts.

When I finally returned to the west coast for my studies, it was with a far greater appreciation of the natural world I had grown up in, and a desire to know it more intimately. I had seen plenty of country in my travels—forty-eight states, nine provinces, and two territories—but there was something special about this place. It had imprinted itself deeply into my being, a mystical connection to the land that spoke to my soul and quietly guided me home.

And so it seems that this natural world has shaped me—affected me in inexplicable ways. Somehow, at some level, there is an understanding of the revelation in creation, and it affects us all. I think St. Paul captures the essence of this in his letter to the Romans in which he writes that God's nature has "been able to be understood and perceived in what He has made." Perhaps this explains that sense of profound reverence and awe we can feel when we enter the wilderness, and why we are so often drawn back to it. For me, it is the underpinning for my deep love of nature and the foundational inspiration behind my photography. It has shaped my character, my personality, my faith—my nature.

This collection of images is different from any I have photographed before. It represents not just a vision of the land but a journey through the world that has surrounded and formed me since childhood. Each image represents not just a place but also an experience that has influenced my life in some way. A mix of the old and the new, as past memories flood in to add depth, colour, and understanding to the scene at hand.

Sometimes we don't truly appreciate or fully understand those experiences of our early years until we are older: learning to fly-fish with my dad on a misty alpine lake, breathing in the dusty-sweet smell of sagebrush after an evening shower, huddling in the family tent while a rip-roaring thunder-and-lighting storm rages outside, snacking on overripe grouse berries high in the subalpine with my mum and grandma, hiking through waves of wildflowers during a marathon backpacking trip, the air thick with the scent of fir and spruce, or getting a finger gobbled by a shy anemone at low tide.

SUCH MOMENTS ARE THE wonderful spice of childhood memories that season our own wilderness experiences as adults, gently influencing who we will become. We should treasure these times, thankful for the blessing of this fragile web of creation that surrounds us—for places like Vancouver, balanced on the edge of wilderness. We should carefully guard these special places as the stewards we were intended to be, for this is part of our very nature.

ACKNOWLEDGEMENTS

A SPECIAL THANKS TO MY WIFE, Myrna, and our new baby, Michael, for their love and great support, especially during the long hours and longer road trips. In the last year, both of them have accompanied me on every shoot. Without Myrna's constant help, encouragement, and patience, many of the images in this book would simply not have been possible. This has truly been a team effort.

Thanks also, to my mum and dad for all their love and support and everything that they have done for me, especially in surrounding me with faith and nature when I was growing up. I would not be who I am today without their love and guidance.

Thanks to Dick Cannings for his great natural insight and his text. Dick was one of my zoology teaching assistants at the University of British Columbia and inspired me to look more deeply into the intricacies of nature.

Thanks also to Rob Sanders of Greystone Books/Douglas & McIntyre for continuing to encourage me in my photography and for publishing my work, to Nancy Flight for her editing help, and to Naomi MacDougall and Peter Cocking for their design and "photographer tolerance."

Also thanks to Kevan Ridgway, Mary Ann Bell, and Leanne Von Hollen at Vancouver Coast and Mountains Tourism for their support of my photography and good friendship. They have all been instrumental in bringing about this book. I believe that tourism is the way of the future for British Columbia, and their role in promoting this spectacular corner of creation to the world is critical today.

Thank you to Paul and Steve Good and all the staff at CustomColor for superb professional E6 transparency film processing and great service. It is much appreciated.

To Dave and the staff at Pentax (Vancouver), thank you for great technical/camera assistance.

And finally, but most importantly, I thank God for all that I have been given. I have been blessed with a wonderful family and place to live. Ultimately, the images on these pages are His work.

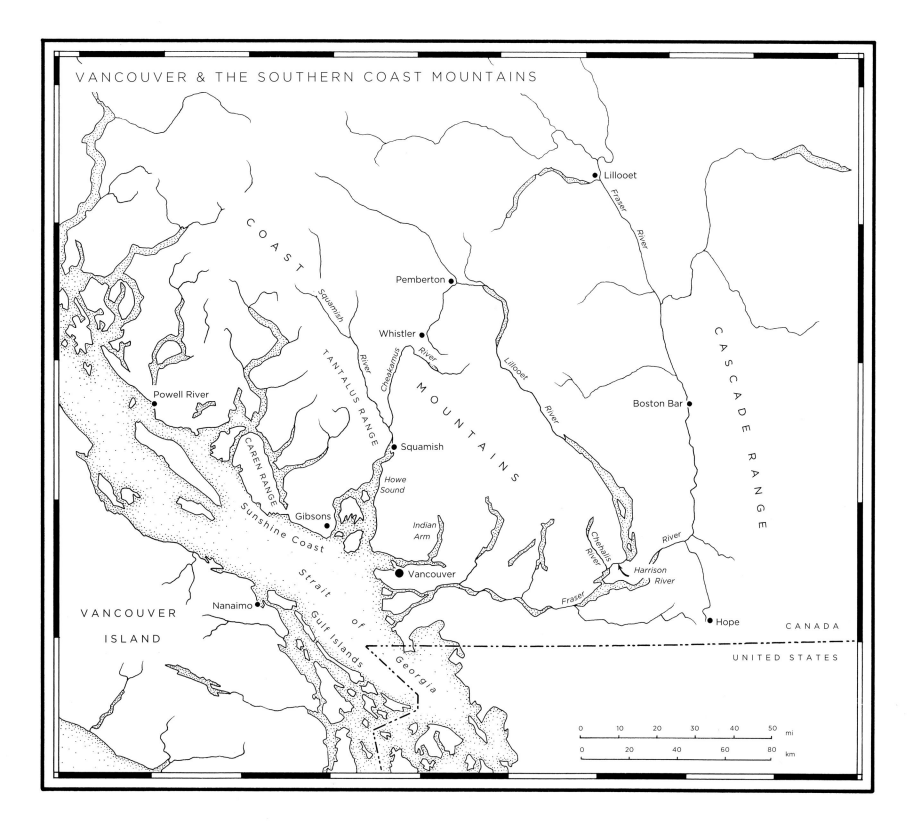

VANCOUVER & THE SOUTHERN COAST MOUNTAINS

Lillooet

COAST

Squamish River

Pemberton

Whistler

Cheakamus River

Lillooet River

Fraser River

Boston Bar

TANTALUS RANGE

M O U N T A I N S

CASCADE RANGE

Powell River

CAREN RANGE

Squamish

Howe Sound

Sunshine Coast

Gibsons

Indian Arm

Chehalis River

Harrison River

River

Vancouver

Fraser

VANCOUVER

Nanaimo

Strait of

Gulf Islands

Georgia

Hope

CANADA

UNITED STATES

ISLAND

| 0 | 10 | 20 | 30 | 40 | 50 | mi |

| 0 | 20 | 40 | 60 | 80 | km |

*W*HEN I MOVED TO VANCOUVER IN 1971
to go to university, I was captivated by the sight from the window of my residence—
massive Douglas-firs silhouetted black against the purple mountains of Vancouver
Island and the orange of the setting sun. I had never lived with trees such as these,
trees that were probably two hundred years old when Captain George Vancouver
first surveyed the local shoreline in 1792. And when the winter monsoons blotted
out the sunsets, I would scramble down the trails to Wreck Beach, the rich aroma
of moss and wet cedar mixing with the tang of the sea, gulls and killdeer crying
behind the steady static of the rain. Spring brought sunny days and early blossoms,
pink salmonberry flowers set against pale green leaves, and cinnamon-coloured
canes. I had come expecting a dreary world of perennially wet concrete but quickly
fell in love with the natural landscape around me.

In Vancouver, more than in most large cities on the planet, nature is every-
where you look. The city is framed on all sides by wild landscapes—to the north
and east by the green wall of the Coast Mountains, to the west by the dark blue
waters of the Strait of Georgia, and to the south by the delta of the mighty Fraser

River. Most cities have parks, but few, if any, have such large and wild natural areas within their urban boundaries as Stanley Park, Pacific Spirit Park, and Lighthouse Park. And within a few hours' drive, there is much more, including the glaciers of the Tantalus Range, the churning waters of Hell's Gate, and the arid sagebrush benchlands at Lillooet.

The natural landscapes around Vancouver are remarkable for their bounty and diversity. The Fraser River feeds the rich waters of the Pacific, which in turn create the winter storms that put the rain into the rain forests of North Vancouver and the snow into Whistler. The abundant water and mild temperatures produce forest growth unequalled anywhere else in the world—the Douglas-firs of the Fraser Valley were likely the largest trees that have ever grown. The vast mud flats of the Fraser are by far the most important feeding ground for migratory and wintering water birds in Canada and are recognized as a critical site for bird conservation on a global scale. Huge runs of spawning salmon attract killer whales in the summer and thousands of bald eagles in the winter. The list of superlatives goes on and on—few cities on Earth can rival Vancouver for its natural heritage.

A crescent moon
setting over Canada
Place at dusk

Just as Vancouver is a relatively young city, its natural setting is relatively young in geological terms. This land became part of North America only a hundred million years ago, as a result of a series of collisions between the continental shelf of North America and several huge pieces of crust called terranes, which created the Coast Mountains and the Cascade Range. Over the past two million years, this land was periodically buried under more than a thousand metres of glacial ice. The last glaciers retreated only twelve thousand years ago, as the climate warmed, leaving a forever-altered landscape. Narrow river valleys had been carved into broad, steep-walled fjords that were flooded by the sea when the ice disappeared, creating deep inlets such as Howe Sound and Indian Arm. Once the ice was gone, the forests and their inhabitants slowly reclaimed the scoured landscape, while fish, including the salmon, recolonized the newborn rivers.

PRECEDING SPREAD

Morning mist
over Stanley Park,
Vancouver's waterfront

RIGHT

The port of Vancouver

FACING PAGE

The Lions Gate Bridge
against morning's
first glow

Mount Baker
silhouetted against
the brilliant palette
of sunrise

Lighthouse Park
and swirling surf
at twilight

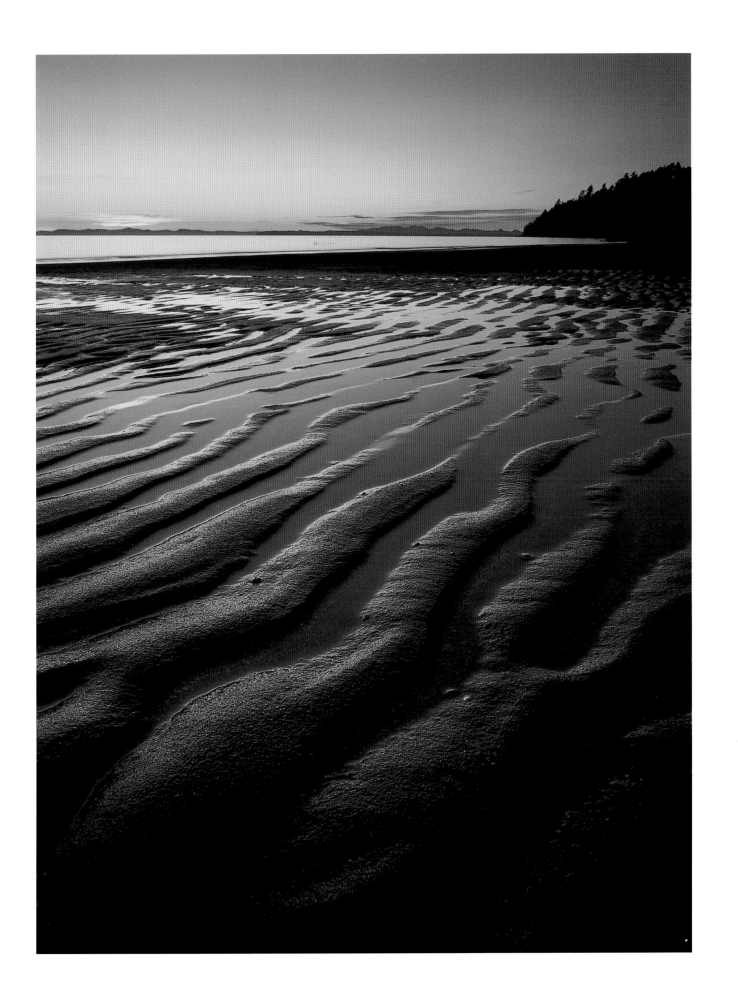

Scalloped sandbars
exposed along
Semiahmoo Bay
at low tide

FOLLOWING PAGE
The Burlington
Northern and Santa
Fe Railway line in
the honeyed light
of morning

"This is something that all

Canadians know,

the FEEL *of the* WILD

even in the heart of the city."

———

WADE DAVIS
Shadows in the Sun

*R*AIN FORESTS ARE CERTAINLY THE feature that most people equate with wild Vancouver. The huge Douglas-firs, red-cedars, and hemlocks that characterize Stanley Park and other pockets of low-elevation old-growth forests once filled the Fraser Valley lowlands. These immense trees thrive in the mild, humid climate. All winter long a stream of Pacific storms sweeps in, driven by the counterclockwise rotation of the Aleutian Low, a storm centre stationed off the coast of Alaska. The storms bring moist, relatively warm air in from the Pacific, often from as far away as Hawaii; these winds are known locally as the "Pineapple Express." As the oceanic air hits the immovable wall of the Coast Mountains, it is forced to rise, cool, and release the water it holds, bringing torrents of rain to coastal forests. Annual precipitation levels increase as you approach the mountains, going from less than a metre (3 feet) at the southern edge of the Fraser Delta to over 3 metres (10 feet) in the upper parts of North Vancouver.

The long, wet winters are mild enough to allow photosynthesis and growth to continue year-round, whereas the summers are relatively cool and sunny—optimal conditions for conifers. The growth is so tremendous that these forests have more

standing biomass—the amount of living material—per hectare than any other ecosystem on Earth. Forest fires occur only every few centuries in this ecosystem, since lightning is rare on the coast and the trees seldom dry out enough to become highly flammable. As a result, these forests can be very old—some have undoubtedly remained undisturbed for more than a millennium, although the individual trees in them are "only" five hundred years old or so. But that life span can create huge trees—many of the veteran Douglas-firs alive today in the few pockets of old-growth forest that remain are more than 80 metres (260 feet) high. Unfortunately, most of these tall trees are gone, cut down in the first few decades of logging in the late 1800s. There are old, anecdotal reports of individual trees more than 120 metres (400 feet) high taken from the Chilliwack area; if these reports are true, these trees would have been the tallest on Earth.

Douglas-firs are the giants of this forest, but they can only germinate in sunlit openings and so commonly establish only after one of the infrequent fires. Once there is a cover of shade, western hemlocks begin to germinate and grow, gradually replacing the Douglas-firs as they age and fall. The hemlocks, with their feathery foliage and delicate, drooping tips, are the dominant species of climax forests. In wetter areas the sweeping branches of western redcedar, which have massive, buttressed trunks, can be seen among the hemlocks. The thick, furrowed bark of Douglas-fir is resistant to most ground fires, whereas the thin-skinned hemlocks and redcedars quickly succumb if fire sweeps through. A pattern of occasional fires thus leaves big Douglas-firs scattered in a landscape of younger trees that germinated after the last fire.

The size of the trees in this forest is impressive, but there is also beauty in the shrubs that grow in the dappled shade on the forest floor. Rufous hummingbirds come back from Mexico in mid-March, their arrival timed perfectly to coincide with the blooming of salmonberries and red flowering currants. In early June the forest is filled with the rising flutelike song of the Swainson's thrush; stories of First Nations people along the northwest coast say that this beautiful song ripens the red and orange salmonberries. Although these evergreen forests do not turn vivid colours in fall as eastern deciduous woodlands do, they are brightened by the flame-coloured leaves of vine maples, which

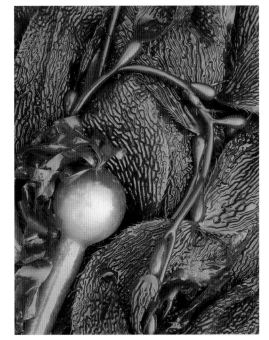

PRECEDING SPREAD, LEFT

Sunset over Francis
Point, on the lower
Sunshine Coast

PRECEDING SPREAD, RIGHT

Sunrise over Lois
Lake near Powell
River, on the upper
Sunshine Coast

RIGHT

Overlooking the lights
of Horseshoe Bay

blaze against the dark background. Even in midwinter several species of forest shrubs—such as salal and red huckleberry—remain green leaved like the coniferous trees above them.

Forests on the Sunshine Coast and the Gulf Islands, lying in the rain shadow of the mountains of Vancouver Island, are drier than those on the mountains rising behind North Vancouver and have a distinctive open character. The twisted trunks of arbutus trees grow amid an understory that is green with grass and bright with flowers in spring. Arbutus is in the heather family, along with salal and huckleberries, and produces bright red berries in the fall, a favourite food of wintering robins and thrushes. Like salal, it keeps its leathery leaves all winter but continually sheds its reddish bark in long, peeling sections.

Black bears and black-tailed deer are common in these forests, but the most abundant and perhaps most ecologically important animals are small creatures such as salamanders, squirrels, and slugs. The lungless salamanders, a family of amphibians adapted to wet forests, thrive in the damp mosses and rotten logs on the forest floor—as many as two hundred can be found in one hectare. The adults

need to stay moist to breathe, for they absorb oxygen through their thin skin rather than through lungs. The female lays a small clutch of large eggs in a humid cavity in an old log, and the tadpoles develop within the eggs, forgoing the aquatic part of the life cycle typical of other salamanders and frogs.

Northern flying squirrels carry on unseen nocturnal lives, feeding on berries, seeds, and fungi. They spend their days deep in cavities of old trees, wrapped in warm nests of lichen and moss. One of their key roles in forest ecology is to spread the spores of mycorrhizal fungi. These fungi form intimate partnerships with tree roots, providing efficient water and nutrient delivery to the tree in return for sugars the tree produces in its leaves. Mycorrhizal fungi produce their spores in mushrooms or in aromatic underground fruiting bodies called truffles. Flying squirrels and other animals eat the mushrooms and truffles, spreading the spores through the forest in their droppings and thus continuing the vital tree/fungus partnerships.

As the clouds sweep higher up the slopes in a winter storm, the moisture in them cools to the point that snowflakes begin to form. The upper altitudes of these coastal mountains are the snowiest places on Earth, with midwinter depths of over

An immature bald eagle feasting on salmon along the Cheakamus River

A Pacific madrone
on Francis Point
stretching out over
Malaspina Strait

5 metres (16 feet) and seasonal accumulations of over 15 metres (50 feet) commonly recorded. The snow comes early in the season, lying on the ground like a giant down quilt and protecting the plants from freezing temperatures. The soil never freezes in these high coastal forests, and a unique community of plants is adapted to these special conditions.

These are the forests of ski hills—Whistler, Cypress Bowl, Grouse, and Mount Seymour. The dominant trees are amabilis fir, mountain hemlock, and yellow cedar, species that cannot tolerate frozen soil but can germinate quickly in the very short growing season. The season available for plant germination is short, not only because of cool summer weather, but because the snow is so deep that it takes months to melt. Despite the early springs along the coast, it is often not until July or even August that all the snow has melted from these high forests.

Because fires are essentially nonexistent in coastal subalpine forests, the trees can be truly ancient. Yellow cedars, in particular, are laced with chemicals that resist fungal attack and repel defoliating insects, allowing the trees to live for many centuries. One yellow cedar on the Caren Range of the Sunshine Coast was 1824 years old.

"We had seen God in His

SPLENDOURS,

heard the text that

Nature renders.

We had reached the naked

SOUL OF MAN."

———

SIR ERNEST SHACKLETON

South: The Story of Shackleton's Last Expedition, 1914–17

Douglas squirrels, small, orange-bellied coastal relatives of the red squirrel, chatter quietly in these forests. Their small size makes them more efficient at feeding on the smaller cones found in coastal hemlock than their interior cousins, which have to contend with large, tough pine cones. Two birds are characteristic of these high forests. The red-breasted sapsucker is a small woodpecker that methodically drills holes in hemlocks and later returns to lap up the sweet sap with its specially designed tongue. Because the sap flows year-round in the snow forests, you can find sapsuckers there all winter, quietly tapping the wet, dark trunks.

You might not expect sea birds to use these forests, but one species, the marbled murrelet, depends on the old-growth stands in coastal forests for its nesting habitat. This starling-sized diving bird, a diminutive relative of the great auk, flies inland on short, stubby wings and lays a single egg on a moss-covered branch high above the ground. The incubating adults and downy nestlings are safe from most predators in these trees, much as their relatives, the murres and auklets, are protected in their nests on seaside cliffs. When the nestling is old enough, it must make its first flight count—it has to fly all the way to the ocean

without crash-landing. These small birds have become increasingly uncommon as logging removes more and more of the stands of large trees they need for nesting, and the birds are now restricted to patches of old-growth forest at high elevations.

As you ascend even higher into the coastal mountains, the forests thin out into strands of trees along ridges or small islands in a sea of flower meadows. Higher still, the trees are reduced to twisted mats that huddle beneath the winter snow pack for protection from winds that pull moisture out of the needles, and the roots are frozen fast in the rocky soil. This is tree line, above which only a few species of plants can survive, tucked into the lee of boulders or forming cushions on the alpine soil. On the coastal side of the mountains, tree line lies at about 1700 metres (5600 feet) elevation, the altitude above which snow accumulation is too great for tree germination. Alpine meadows on the coast are dominated by cold-tolerant sedges and heaths such as blueberries, huckleberries, and heathers. Summer colours are subdued, but the meadows glow fire-red in fall as the blueberry leaves turn colour.

"There is something bigger than fact:

the underlying spirit, all it stands for,

the MOOD, *the* VASTNESS,

the WILDNESS… *the* ETERNAL

big spaceness of it. Oh the WEST!

I'm of it and I love it."

———

EMILY CARR
Hundreds and Thousands

Few animals live in the true alpine, the rocks above tree line. Horned larks come here in summer, tucking their cuplike nests behind the protection of a rock or clump of windblown grass. The males pour out their tinkling songs high in the dark blue sky, then plummet to Earth to perch on prominent rocks and survey their territories. The only bird to live at these altitudes year-round is the white-tailed ptarmigan, a diminutive grouse that is the colour of a lichen-covered rock in summer and snow-white in winter. The cryptic coloration of ptarmigans is legendary; I have on occasion sat next to a small flock for several minutes, not realizing they were there until they got up to leave, softly cackling as they crept away.

On the eastern slopes, tree line rises to about 2100 metres (6900 feet), the altitude at which the warm summer growing season becomes too short for tree germination. Subalpine meadows on these slopes are rich in mountain flowers, great sweeps of colour that paint the mountains in two distinct waves each summer. The first blooms come just as the snow melts; some of the blossoms impatiently burst through the last bit of snow. Fields of creamy anemones and butter-yellow glacier lilies carpet these moist meadows. As the soil dries and summer reaches its zenith in July, a second wave of flowers appears—blue lupines, red paintbrush, yellow arnica, white valerian, and more. Along moss-lined snowmelt streams tumbling through the meadows bloom bouquets of brook saxifrage, pink elephant's head, and snapdragon-like clusters of monkey flowers.

Everything here must take advantage of the short summers to survive. Pikas—essentially small-footed, short-eared rabbits—scamper from flower meadows to safety in the jumble of rocks on scree slopes. There they lay out grasses and flowers in hay piles on large, sunny rocks, then store the vegetation under rocks for winter food. Pikas are ever alert for danger, and their loud *enk!* calls are an integral part of the alpine soundscape. Marmots graze on grass and flowers as well, putting on fat to get them through the long alpine winter. True hibernators, marmots spend eight months each year below ground in a state of suspended animation, waiting for the warm days of late May. Their loud, piercing warning calls gave them the nickname "whistler," which in turn became the name of the well-known mountain and ski resort.

"British Columbia is HEAVEN.

It trembles within me

and pains with its wonder

as when a child I first awakened

to the song of the EARTH AT HOME.*"*

———

F.H. VARLEY

"The Paintings and Drawings of F.H. Varley," *Canadian Art*

High-elevation forests on the eastern, leeward side of the coastal mountains are quite different from the snow forests that face the sea. The clouds that buried the western slopes in snow have little moisture left in them after they crest the peaks, so snow on eastern slopes is rarely more than 2 or 3 metres (6 to 10 feet) deep. The continental side of the mountains also has a correspondingly more continental climate. Without the moderating influence of the Pacific, air temperatures are lower in winter and higher in summer. So the trees and other plants here don't have to contend with lingering snow packs but are faced with early frosts and quickly frozen soil.

Common trees here are Engelmann spruce and subalpine fir, species that dominate the mountain forests from British Columbia to New Mexico. Fire is a big player in this landscape, where the hot summer sun dries the forest and fuels afternoon thunderstorms. The mature fir and spruce burn quickly and cannot easily re-germinate in the open, sunny habitat created by the fire. Instead, they are replaced by a thick forest of young lodgepole pine. Lodgepole pine has special cones that remain closed throughout the life of the tree but crack open when

Sword ferns

and vine maples

near Squamish

A massive western
redcedar and
devil's club,
Sims Creek Valley

"*It is dark in the* LOST LAGOON,

And gone are the depths of haunting blue,

The grouping gulls, and the old canoe,

The singing firs, and the dusk and—you,

And gone is the GOLDEN MOON."

———————

PAULINE JOHNSON
The Lost Lagoon

heated by fire, releasing a shower of seeds after the flames pass. As the pine forest matures and naturally thins itself, fir and spruce seedlings germinate in the shady understory; over a century or so, they will gradually outgrow the pines to create a climax forest that will last until the next fire.

Red squirrels are conspicuous in these forests; you are rarely out of earshot of scolding squirrels while hiking through pine and spruce. They are guarding their middens—storehouses of seed-filled cones that will get them through the long winter.

Below the dense forests of spruce and fir on the eastern ranges of the Coast Mountains, the forests open up into Douglas-fir woodlands, a sunlit forest with a bright green pinegrass understory. These Douglas-firs are considered a different subspecies from their coastal counterparts; the mature trees are more flat topped and have a greyer foliage. The thick, dark bark of older trees is spangled with star-tling chartreuse clumps of wolf lichen.

Winter snow packs are relatively light on these slopes, making them critical winter range for mule deer. Another characteristic denizen is the flammulated owl,

Purple monkey flowers and dwarf alpine fireweed gracing the headwater valley of Wave Creek

an insectivorous bird the size of a small coffee mug that returns to these forests each spring from wintering grounds in Mexico and northern Central America. Warm May nights are punctuated by the males' soft *boo-boot!* calls as they advertise their territories and chosen nest sites—woodpecker holes in old snags.

As you hike down one of these eastern ridges, the forest opens even more and the dark Douglas-fir trunks mix with the warm orange trunks of ponderosa pines. Lower still the woodlands are a parkland of large pines with an understory of blue-bunch wheatgrass. This is the driest forest of British Columbia, with an annual precipitation of about 30 centimetres (12 inches). The summers are so hot and dry—Lytton holds the record for the highest temperature in the province, 44.4°C (112°F)—that trees can only germinate in exceptionally wet, cool years.

The seedlings quickly send down deep taproots, and older trees can have lateral roots that spread more than 40 metres (130 feet) from the trunk to gather scarce water from occasional rainstorms. Ponderosa pines are beautiful trees, with their colourful, jigsaw puzzle bark, long, graceful needles, and big round cones. Naturalist John Muir thought they made the finest wind music of all trees, and their scent

is gorgeous. Next time you find yourself beside a ponderosa pine, sniff the bark—it has the wonderful aroma of vanilla.

Ecologists call these dry forests fire maintained—they have evolved with frequent forest fires that burn away small trees and shrubs every twenty years or so. The mature trees have thick bark that resists burning; some ecologists even believe that the large trees encourage ground fires with the deep carpet of flammable needles they drop to the ground.

The flat benches along the Fraser River north of Boston Bar—terraces formed against the valley glaciers as they melted at the end of the Pleistocene—are covered with sagebrush and bunchgrasses. This is the lower tree line, where summers are too hot and dry for tree germination—Ashcroft has had as little as 7 centimetres (2¾ inches) of precipitation in one year, but the average is about 20 centimetres (18 inches). This is semidesert country, with brittle prickly-pear cactus and rattlesnakes. Bighorn sheep find sanctuary in the steep bluffs above the Fraser River, venturing out onto the grassy benches for grazing.

Most of the plant growth here takes place in spring, when the soil is moist from snowmelt and frequent rain showers maintain that moisture through the warm days. Sagebrush buttercups carpet the ground in March, followed by a series of other wildflower species, culminating in the delicate mauve blooms of the mariposa lily in early July. After that the grasslands turn golden as they dry in the summer sun, the plants storing nutrients in their root systems until the following spring.

The Fraser River flows through this arid landscape, carrying the rainfall and snowmelt of much of British Columbia. From a watershed of more than 200,000 square kilometres (77,000 square miles) the Fraser flows for more than 1000 kilometres (600 miles) to the sea, sending an average of almost 3000 cubic metres (800,000 gallons) of water per second into the Pacific. The flow peaks at more than 10,000 cubic metres (2.6 million gallons) per second in June as the snows from the high Rockies melt.

The Fraser and other British Columbia rivers not only carry nutrients to the ocean but also provide a pathway for marine nutrients to return to the mountain streams. This return is carried out by the Pacific salmon—sockeye, chinook, pink, chum, and steelhead—as they return to their natal rivers to spawn. Some, such

"*To describe the* BEAUTIES

of this region will,

on some future occasion,

be a very grateful task

to the pen of a skilled

PANEGYRIST."

———

CAPTAIN GEORGE VANCOUVER

A Voyage of Discovery to the North Pacific Ocean & Round the World

as the coho spawning in the Capilano River between West Vancouver and North Vancouver, travel only a few kilometres, and up to 10 million pink salmon spawn in the Fraser River below Hope. Many salmon go much farther; some chinook salmon swim almost the entire length of the Fraser to spawn and die in the shadow of Mount Robson, the highest peak of the Canadian Rockies.

The dead and dying salmon provide life for a myriad of creatures along the rivers. Bears, eagles, and gulls flock to each run in turn to feed on the bounty. Some of these congregations, especially those at midwinter runs of chum salmon along the coast, are truly spectacular. The Squamish and Cheakamus rivers at Brackendale attract more than three thousand bald eagles in December and January; these birds fly in from all over western North America for the event. The Harrison and Chehalis rivers in the Fraser Valley draw smaller but still impressive numbers of eagles. Smaller animals come in as well. Dippers, grey birds the size (and more or less the shape) of tennis balls, bob up and down on the rocks, diving in to search for salmon eggs and newly hatched fry. Riverside animals are not the only organisms to benefit from the salmon; the carcasses carried into the forest by bears provide a significant fertilizer boost for the huge redcedars and hemlocks along their banks.

FACING PAGE

A hoary marmot,
Whistler's namesake,
gives a piercing
alarm whistle

LEFT

A pair of Columbian
ground squirrels
nuzzling along the
Nicomen Lake trail,
Manning Park

In spring the Fraser hosts a spawning run of a different sort—the eulachon run. Millions of these small silver fish leave the ocean to spawn between Mission and Chilliwack. The sheer numbers of the highly nutritious eulachon attract harbour seals and sea lions into the river—some go upstream as far as the Pitt River, the limit of tidal activity on the river. The eulachon were a dietary mainstay of First Nations cultures along the coast, and eulachon grease was widely traded with Interior peoples.

The Fraser meets the ocean along the southern edge of Vancouver, depositing tonnes of silt at its mouth each year and providing local marine life with a rich source of nutrients at its mouth. The eelgrass beds of Roberts Bank—north of the Tsawwassen ferry terminal—are a critical nursery ground for many young salmon and other fish. The mud flats of the Fraser delta may not look like much at first sight, but they are the most important feeding ground for migrating shorebirds and wintering waterfowl in Canada. Almost the entire world population of western sandpipers stops here in spring and fall; sometimes thirty thousand or more of these tiny travellers can be seen wheeling in tight formation over the flats as they

continue their journey. In November they are replaced by similar flocks of dunlin, an Arctic sandpiper that spends the winter on the delta.

My favourite wildlife spectacle in the Vancouver area is the huge number of snow geese that spend the winter on the Fraser delta, primarily on Westham Island. They begin to arrive in late September, and their numbers peak in late October and November. Then swirling white clouds of geese—tens of thousands of them—can be seen over the mud flats, their bugling calls mingling in a constant high chord that fills the late-fall air. Most of these geese move south in midwinter, but they return in February before departing for the Arctic in April.

In the heart of the delta is Burns Bog, the largest raised bog on the west coast of North America. The bog is home to many plants and animals normally found far to the north, for the bog's harsh environment is very similar to that of the acidic peatlands that cover much of northern Canada. Dragonflies typical of northern ponds hover over the pools of Burns Bog, and a relict population of sandhill cranes nests there.

The Fraser River plume spreads across the Strait of Georgia, a milky brown stain on the dark green water. The nutrients carried by the plume mix with the marine waters as the tidal currents flow across the river mouth. Twice daily the tide pours in through the narrow passes between the Gulf Islands, then retreats to the open sea again. This tidal mixing and the rich waters of the rivers give the Vancouver coastline a wealth of sea life. Most of us see only what is on top of the waters, but that is impressive enough—pods of killer whales chasing down salmon as they make for the mouth of the river, clouds of gulls diving into water churning with a massive school of herring. If you venture beneath these waters, you will see one of the most diverse marine ecosystems on Earth—undersea cliffs cloaked with sea anemones, forests of kelp hiding flickering schools of perch, giant Pacific octopus slipping into dark lairs.

*V*ANCOUVER WAS A WILDER PLACE TWO hundred years ago. The ancient trees stood tall in the green forests, and great salt marshes filled the Fraser Delta. Today most of the old forests are gone, replaced by dense second-growth stands that lack the structural and species diversity of their predecessors. The spotted owl was once common in Vancouver forests, hunting flying squirrels by night and resting in cavities of the huge trees by day. Now there are only a handful of these chocolate-brown night birds left in Canada. The Fraser Delta has been dyked and drained, its marshes turned into cranberry farms and shopping malls, the waters of the river mixing with sewage and industrial outflows.

But there is yet hope—the mountains and seas around Vancouver are still wild and wonderful places. There are no hydroelectric dams on the main channel of the Fraser River, and many of its salmon runs are still reasonably healthy. Humpback whales, once a common sight off Vancouver but hunted to extirpation a century ago, are being seen again in the Strait of Georgia. But the great hope for the wildness of Vancouver is in its people, famous for their love of nature and the outdoors. We must realize what a treasure we have in this great city and the world that surrounds it so that its wildness will still be here centuries from today.

RIGHT

Looking down on
the snaking channel
of the Fraser River
near Harrison Mills

FACING PAGE

Mist shrouding the
Golden Ears, the
Serpentine River
near Cloverdale

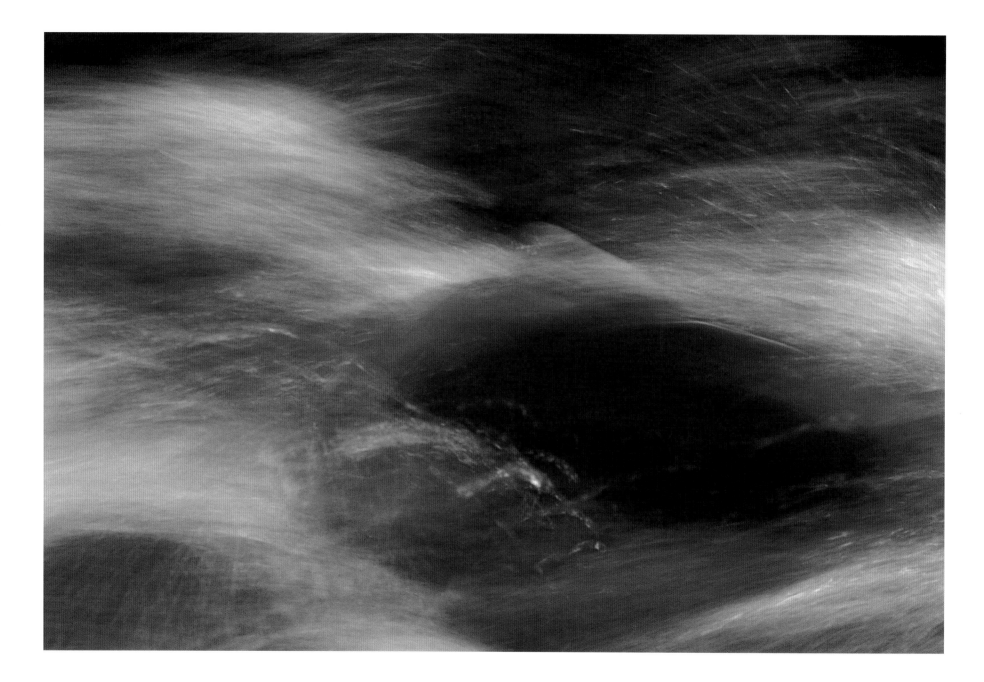

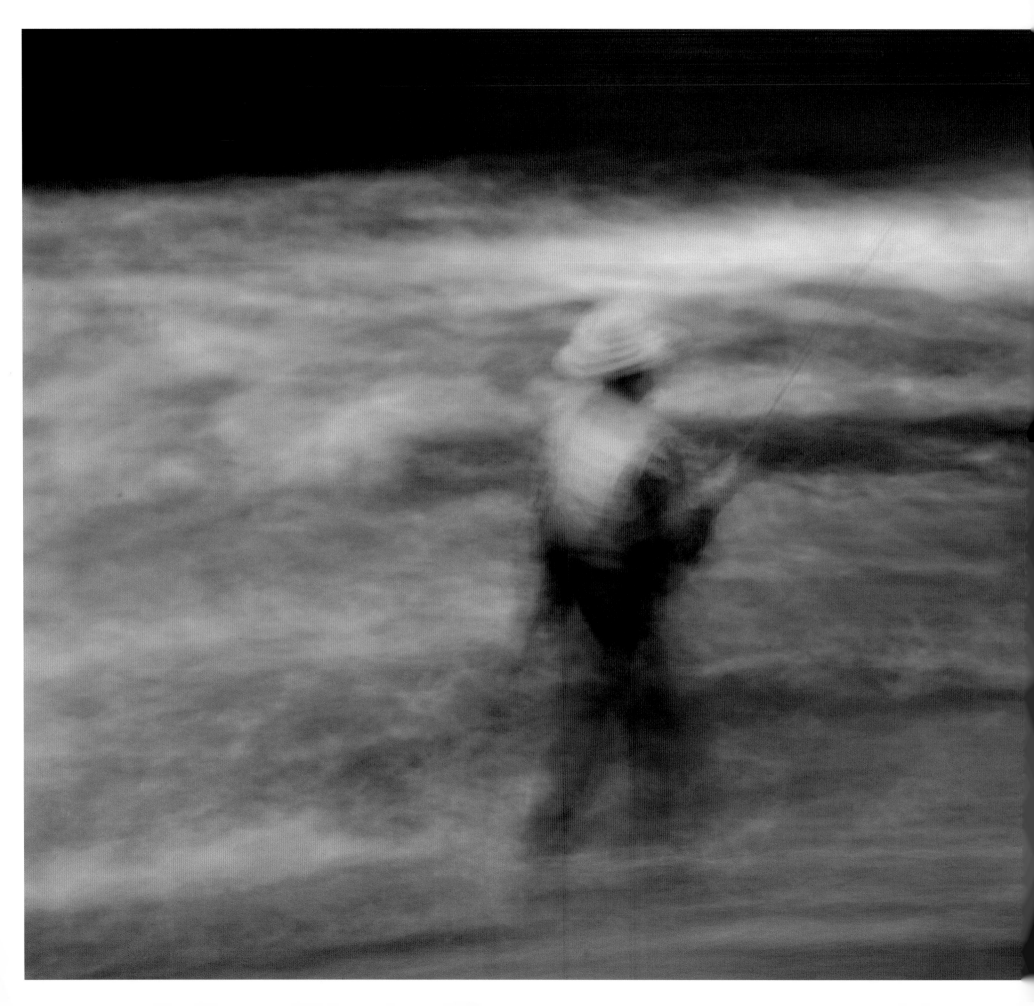

"I want to be a part of the river

and all my surroundings,

N O T *a stranger thrusting in*

upon them . . . I want to feel the river

about me and to fill my mind

with the infinity of lights that break

from its S U R F A C E *and its* D E P T H S *."*

———————

RODERICK HAIG-BROWN
The Master and His Fish

Looking out over
Montagu Channel
near Porteau Cove
at last light

RIGHT

A flock of snow
geese resting along
the Fraser River
estuary near Ladner

FACING PAGE

Tidal channels criss-
crossing Boundary
Bay at low tide

FOLLOWING SPREAD

First light pouring
into the Fraser Valley
near Langley as the
sun crests over
the shoulder of
Mount Baker

"After the RAIN

the grass will shed its moisture,

the fog will lift from the trees,

a new light will brighten the sky

and PLAY *in the* DROPS

that hang on all things.

Your HEART *will beat out*

a new gladness

—if you let it HAPPEN*."*

CHIEF DAN GEORGE
Words to a Grandchild

BELOW

A western sandpiper
admiring itself in
a tidal pool near
Boundary Bay

RIGHT

Waves of snow geese
heading for the safety
of the Fraser Delta
salt marshes at dusk,
Reifel Island

PRECEDING SPREAD

Spring mist filtering
through valley bot-
tom trees along the
Campbell River

RIGHT

Bridal Veil Falls
cascading in curtains
of phantom blue,
near Rosedale

FACING PAGE

Frosted river rocks
along the Lillooet
River at the north
end of Harrison Lake

FOLLOWING SPREAD

A stand of giant
old-growth western
redcedars, Chilliwack
River Ecological
Reserve

"*The* INTRICACIES *of* LIFE

in an old-growth forest

are far more complex

and much less understood

than life in a large city."

———

BRISTOL FOSTER
The West Coast: Canada's Rain Forest

PRECEDING SPREAD, LEFT

A yellow pine chipmunk
nibbling a seed head
high in the subalpine

PRECEDING SPREAD, RIGHT

Vine maples in brilliant
orange and yellow along
the Skagit River

LEFT

Horses grazing
"The Flats" between
the Serpentine and
Nicomeckl rivers

FACING PAGE

Mount Baker in a
sea of blue lupines

RIGHT

Daisies in bloom
along Vancouver's
waterfront

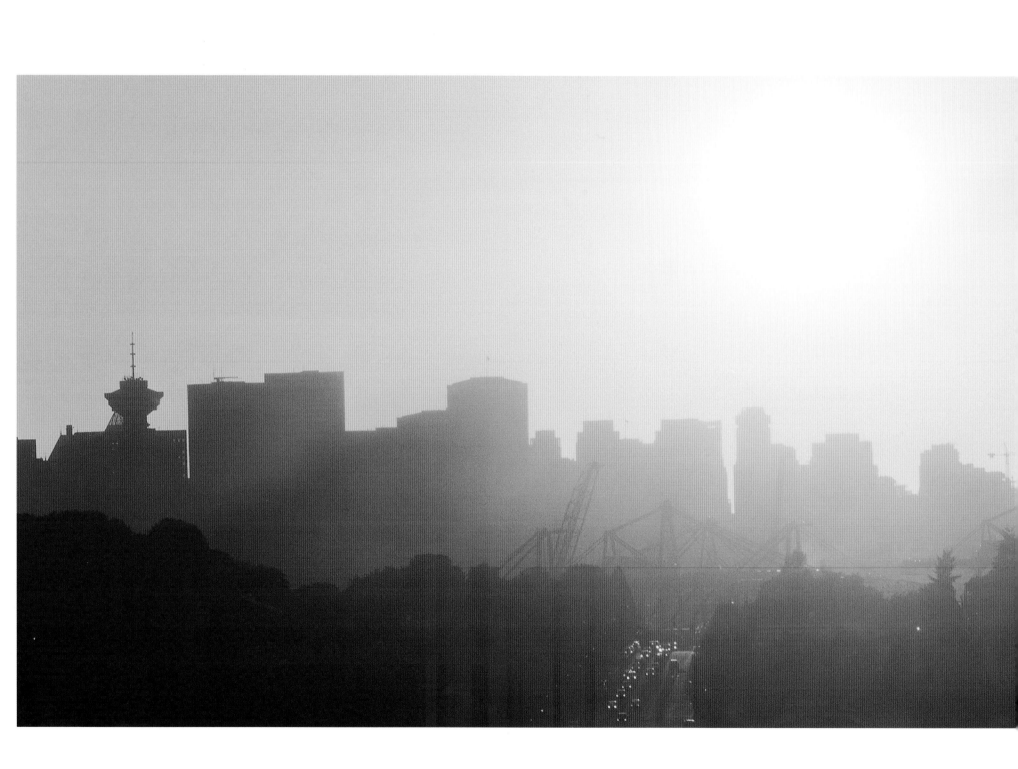

TECHNICAL NOTES

THE IMAGES IN THIS BOOK WERE SHOT predominantly with medium- and large-format cameras. A Pentax 67 camera was used extensively for many images, along with 45, 50 (specially adapted), 55, 90, and 200 mm lenses, and has proved to be a superb field camera. A Toyo 45A 4×5 field camera was also used, along with 47, 90, and 150 mm lenses. Nikon 35 mm equipment was used for most wildlife and long telephoto shots, including an 80–200 mm zoom lens and 500 and 600 mm telephoto lenses.

Ektachrome 100 VS and Fuji Velvia transparency film were used for most images in the book because of their excellent colour saturation throughout the spectrum. Polarizing filters were used to remove reflections where appropriate, and a split neutral density filter was used occasionally to balance high-contrast situations.

No images in this book were digitally enhanced or manipulated in any way. They remain as I photographed them.